50
WAYS
TO BE A
GREENER
SHOPPER

SIÂN BERRY

ABOUT
THE AUTHOR

Siân Berry is the Green Party's candidate for London Mayor in 2008 and is a founder of the successful campaign group, the Alliance Against Urban 4x4s.

Siân was one of the Green Party's Principal Speakers until September 2007 and was previously national Campaigns Co-ordinator. She stood in the Hampstead and Highgate constituency in the 2005 General Election and has campaigned in her local area for more affordable housing and, nationally, to promote renewable energy and local shops.

Famous for the mock parking tickets created by Siân in 2003, the Alliance Against Urban 4x4s is now a national campaign and the group recently celebrated persuading the current Mayor of London to propose a higher congestion charge for big 4x4 vehicles and other gas-guzzlers.

Siân studied engineering at university and her professional background is in communications. These skills give her a straightforward and accessible approach to promoting green issues, focusing on what people can do today to make a difference, and on what governments need to do to make greener lives easier for everyone.

As spokesperson for the Alliance and a well-known Green Party figure, Siân has received wide coverage in national and international newspapers and has appeared on numerous TV and radio shows, from Radio 4's *Today* programme to *Richard and Judy*. Her calm, cheerful and persuasive advocacy has stimulated a lively public debate about 4x4s, and has helped to raise the environment further up the public agenda.

50

WAYS

TO BE A

GREENER
SHOPPER

SIÂN BERRY

Kyle Cathie Ltd

First published in Great Britain in 2008 by
Kyle Cathie Ltd
122 Arlington Road, London NW1 7HP
general.enquiries@kyle-cathie.com
www.kylecathie.com

10 9 8 7 6 5 4 3 2 1

978-1-85626-774-8

Editorial Director: Muna Reyal
Illustrator and Designer: Aaron Blecha
Production Director: Sha Huxtable

A Cataloguing In Publication record for this title is
available from the British Library.

Colour reproduction by Scanhouse
Printed and bound in Italy by Amadeus

Printed on 100% recycled paper

HAVE NOTHING IN YOUR HOUSE THAT YOU DO NOT KNOW TO BE USEFUL, OR DO NOT BELIEVE TO BE BEAUTIFUL

WILLIAM MORRIS

50 WAYS TO...

In the home, in the garden, at the shops, at work and on the move, this series of books contains a wide range of simple ways to live a greener life, whatever your situation. Each book has 50 easy, affordable and creative tips to help you live more lightly on the planet.

There are many ways to be green that don't need a big investment of money, time, effort or space. Saving energy also saves money on your bills, and eco-friendly products don't have to be high-tech or expensive.

Any size garden – or even a window box – can be a haven for wildlife and provide useful low-maintenance crops that save on imported fruit and vegetables. And those of us living in towns and cities should know that urban living can provide some of the lowest-carbon lifestyles around.

The *50 ways* series has been written by Siân Berry: Green Party candidate for Mayor of London in 2008 and a founder of the successful campaign group, the Alliance Against Urban 4x4s. She shares her experiences to demonstrate how you can reduce your carbon footprint, stay ahead of fashion and enjoy life without sacrifice.

Siân says, 'Being green is not about giving everything up; it's about using things cleverly and creatively to cut out waste. In these books, I aim to show you that a greener life without fuss is available to everyone.'

INTRODUCTION

We all have to go shopping in order to live. Food is a daily necessity; clothes and personal care are crucial for our well being; our homes need furnishings; our children need all kinds of creature comforts; and enjoying special occasions like Christmas, birthdays and weddings seems to mean a longer shopping list every time.

With protecting the environment and the effects of climate change becoming more of a concern every day, we are starting to realise that we will also have to change our shopping habits if our efforts to save the planet in other ways, such as cutting down on energy use and reducing travel miles, are going to work.

The problem is that everything we buy has an impact on the environment. Making things in factories, growing food and transporting products all use up the fossil fuels that cause climate change. Many products are made in ways that create pollution, and when they go down the drain or fill up landfill sites after use, they can also cause problems.

For all these reasons, shopping has become an ethical minefield for keen greens like me. What can I buy that will save resources, rather than destroy a rainforest or use up vast amounts of oil? Which is best – organic or local? Why is there no Fairtrade coffee in my local supermarket? And why can't I find long-lasting products that don't break down as soon as their guarantee expire?

As a member of the Green Party, I am working to make big changes to the way our society is run. My aim is to make the greenest and most ethical options the easiest and cheapest options for everyone. But this isn't the case yet, so I am often asked by friends, colleagues and people on the street for tips on the best things to buy.

Finding out the impact of different purchases hasn't been simple. Labels don't tell us much, shops and producers have been slow to give us information about the things they sell, and the number of campaigners asking us to boycott companies and products makes it seem like everything on the shelves causes huge problems.

However, there are some basic principles we can bring to the process of seeking out greener products. Repair, reuse and recycle are the green 'three Rs' and they come in handy at the shops too. We can shop less by buying things to last, repair and reuse the things we have, and buy recycled, organic and local products whenever we can.

In these pages, you will find these principles applied across a wide range of shopping situations. The result is 50 of the best tips I have found for greener shopping, from great ideas for reducing the amount of stuff you need to buy, to a host of alternative products that will help to reduce your ecological footprint without spending a fortune.

Lots of the ideas cover ways to save time and money by reducing your shopping needs, but there are also plenty of tips on how to find quality second-hand and recycled goods, and how to find new products with a lower impact on the planet. Since shopping trips are often prompted by special events such as birthdays, weddings and Christmas, there are also some great alternative gift and leisure ideas that I have picked up over the years, as well as some greener ways to feed, wash and clothe the smallest members of your family.

I hope that the advice in this book helps to bring some clarity to the thorny issue of ethical consumption, and that it inspires you to try some new ways to shop in future.

THINK LOCAL

Shopping locally, or buying goods grown and made in your local area, brings lots of green benefits.

As small local shops become scarce and out-of-town supermarkets take a bigger share of the money we spend, travelling to and from the shops takes up a lot of time and generates plenty of carbon. Spending more time in local shops helps us cut down on the carbon footprint of shopping trips.

But it's not just getting to the shops that adds to the carbon footprint of our shopping. The distance many goods travel to reach the shops can also be enormous.

The contents of one typical shopping basket have been found to have covered more than 100,000 miles on their way to the shelves. Food miles aren't written on the label, but here are some simple ways to reduce the amount of travelling done by your groceries on the way to your cupboards.

1 USE YOUR LOCAL SHOPS

Shopping locally has lots of positive effects, not just green benefits.

Local high streets and shopping parades are vital to the health of our communities. An attractive range of local shops provides a place to meet and socialise as well as stock up.

With the owners more likely to live locally, the money you spend in local shops helps the local economy, too. Research has shown that money spent in locally owned businesses can circulate in the area three times before disappearing into the economy at large, whereas most spending done in chain stores leaves the area almost immediately.

People without cars often rely on having a good range of local shops. Pensioners and parents need a local chemist and post office, and can't easily reach out-of-town shopping centres.

Small shops are also lower energy users than big stores with their open freezers, bright lights left on all day and night, open doors with fierce heat curtains, and harsh air-conditioning inside. Per square metre of shopping space, an independent greengrocer consumes up to three times less energy than a supermarket.

A major green benefit of supporting your local shops is in reducing travel by car. In the UK now, about one in ten journeys by car and 5 per cent of all mileage is to buy food. So, walking to local shops whenever you can makes a big difference in reducing congestion, cutting your fuel costs and increasing the exercise you get.

If you can't get everything you need nearby, switching just some of your shopping to your local shops can still help rebuild the vitality of your area. Why not start buying a few regular items from local independent shops and then asking them to stock more of the other things you need? The owner of a local shop may be more likely to respond to customer requests than a manager in a chain store.

2 SHOP FOR LOCAL GOODS

The number of food miles travelled goes up every year. Farming and food are responsible for around a third of all goods transported on our roads and, between 1968 and 1998, trade in food between countries increased almost twice as fast as the world's population.

These days 85 per cent of cut flowers in the UK are imported. Vegetables grown in one area are often transported hundreds of miles to a central factory for packaging before being sent to shops all over the country, and beyond.

Differences in labour costs play their part, too. Goods may be transported to faraway countries for packing in a factory with lower wages, if the cost of transport is less than the savings made this way.

A further problem is the way we are encouraged to buy the same range of products all year round. This can lead to long journeys by air for fruit and vegetables being grown in a different season on the other side of the world.

Although you can find the country of origin on most products, the full distance travelled by your shopping is not easy to calculate when you are in a hurry to buy something for dinner. However, following these simple tips should make a big difference in cutting down the globetrotting elements of your shopping.

• Eat in season, avoid salads in the winter for instance, and eat more root vegetables instead. In summer and autumn, make sure you eat lots of abundant local fruit – and why not use it to make jam for the winter, too?

• Use local food providers, such as organic box schemes and farmers' markets. These will always stock the freshest seasonal goods.

• Go for imported produce that is likely to have come by ship, not by plane. Soft fruits and salad vegetables are often flown in so avoid these out of season. To see you through the cold months, choose fruits that will stay fresh over longer journeys by ship, including bananas and oranges, which are rarely air freighted.

3 SUPPORT THE SPECIALISTS

Imagine going into a supermarket and asking for advice on finding a suitable book for your nephew, how best to cook a cut of meat, or how to find an energy-efficient television. You might strike it lucky, but the chances are you'd get no help at all.

The fact is, with supermarkets expanding their range of goods fast, supermarket staff can't be expected to know about all the products in their stores, and this isn't good for customers.

In contrast, a local butcher, bookshop owner or electrical shop assistant is likely to be able to give useful advice on all the products they sell. They can help you to choose better, as well as dig out the best bargains.

Many specialist shopkeepers are also happy to order things they don't have in stock and have them ready for you a few days later. That personal touch makes all the difference.

GET ONLINE

The internet is a great resource for the greener shopper. Where specialist local shops have disappeared, the advice they used to give is now easy to find online.

Greener products can be researched and compared without clocking up extra travel miles visiting different shops, and the market for second-hand goods has blossomed again, thanks to auction and exchange sites such as eBay and Freecycle.

Although it would be great to have all this going on in our local towns, if you get online today, a greener shopping future can look closer than you think.

4 HUNT OUT ECO-PRODUCTS

One classic bit of green advice has always been to change your light bulbs to low-energy models. I switched most of my ordinary bulbs years ago, but given my liking for vintage home furnishings, until recently I still had several lamps with smaller bulb fittings, which I hadn't been able to change.

As a good greenie, I was finding it very frustrating going into shop after shop and seeing just one standard, low-energy light bulb on sale. In fact I almost gave up.

But then someone told me about an online shop selling only green products and suggested I have a look. A quick search on their website led me to greener light bulbs in every kind of size and fitting I needed.

The high street, with its big chains and long-term buying schedules, isn't changing very quickly. However, the range of green things available online is increasing fast – from greener home products to clothes, shoes and even environmentally friendly pet food. When something green comes onto the market, you're guaranteed to find it online first.

See the online shops and websites at the back of this book for details on where to start.

5 START DOWNLOADING

Another kind of fast-growing online shopping is the downloading of music and films. Lots of illegal file-sharing goes on, but if you don't want to take the risk of being targeted by the copyright police, there are still lots of places where you can legally download music and films.

This often costs much less than buying a CD or DVD from the shops. The companies selling downloads make savings on packaging and transport, and a lot of these are passed onto you. The planet benefits, too, from not having to provide precious resources (mainly oil-based plastics) just to transfer digital ones and zeros to your computer.

Downloading doesn't have to mean watching films on your computer screen. I have set up my computer to pass sound and video through my DVD player into my TV (it only takes a few minutes to work out which wires plug in where), so there's no difference between a real DVD or a download in the quality of what I eventually watch.

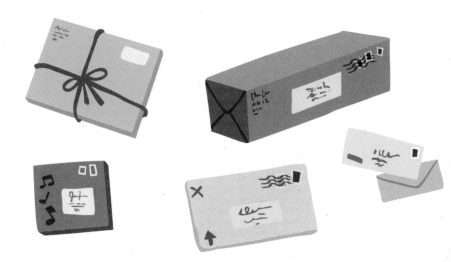

Similarly, if you have an MP3 player, there's no reason at all why you should buy physical CDs, but if you do want a copy on disc, you can always burn one.

If you'd rather stick with traditional discs, there are other useful options available, such as online rental services where you pay a subscription and borrow a range of titles, which you receive and send back by mail. This again saves on the production of discs, as well as shelf space at home for films you will only watch once.

Of course, borrowing from a local library involves even less transport, so check these out too – they may have a wider range of items than you think.

6 FIND SECOND-HAND BARGAINS

Reuse is one of the green 'three Rs' and buying something second-hand is a great way to make resources go further – and get a bargain in the process.

The internet has taken over from newspaper classified adverts as the best place to find and sell used items.

There are various approaches taken by different sites, and no doubt someone will come up with an even better one soon.

Craigslist operates exactly like normal classified ads, providing a place for people to advertise second-hand goods for sale. It has a very simple browsing system and search facility. Remember to choose your nearest local site before browsing to find what you need close to home.

Ebay is the most famous example of an auction-based site. You can find almost anything here, and usually you have to put in a bid for the items you want and hope no-one beats your price before the deadline. This can be a bit frustrating sometimes, but I know several people who are now masters at winning online auctions and get a wide range of bargains.

Freecycle is a network that helps people give away unwanted goods to people in their local area. It specialises in creating local links, and you generally have to register with a local forum to exchange messages and see what's available near to you. It's also a great way to get rid of things you don't need. If you're setting up a home or office, it's well worth joining your local Freecycle group to pick up good-quality items for literally nothing, saving money for other expenses.

CUT THE OIL CONTENT OF YOUR FOOD

I'm not talking about vegetable oil here. The amount of fossil fuels consumed in the production of food might surprise you.

In 2000 a blockade by protesters angry about the price of petrol caused fuel shortages in the UK and, in London, we were shocked afterwards to discover how close we came to finding our supermarket shelves completely empty. But it's not just transport that uses oil. From fertilisers to pesticides, from farm machinery to factories making processed food, our whole food chain depends on vast quantities of oil.

Packaging plays its part as well. If you buy a tin of vegetables, more than a third of the energy required to produce it can be used up producing the steel tin alone.

The carbon dioxide emissions from all this oil really add up. The emissions caused by producing, processing and transporting the food for a typical family is more than 8 tonnes a year.

There has been a huge decline in the amount of real cooking done at home in recent years. Our busier lives have helped reduce the number of families eating together and reduced the time we spend preparing food. The average time taken to prepare an evening meal has dropped from 90 minutes in the 1980s to just 20 minutes today.

Eating local, organic and unpackaged food can be much less energy intensive, and isn't hard to do. Read these tips for some easy ways to make meals that are lighter on oil.

7 EAT ORGANIC

Organic farms use 50–70 per cent less energy to produce food than conventional farming. So by choosing organic food, you are reducing your carbon footprint as well as cutting down on water and soil pollution.

Finding organic alternatives has never been easier, with most supermarkets and local shops, butchers and greengrocers stocking a range of organically grown or reared produce. Reducing the impact of your food, then, can be as simple as looking for these products on the shelves.

However, watch out for organic food that has travelled a long way. In the UK, the chances of organic fruit being imported are very high while home production struggles to catch up with demand, whereas organic eggs, milk and poultry are almost all sourced from farms closer to home.

The country of origin is marked on most fresh foods, so keep an eye on the food miles when choosing organic and you won't be making one environmental problem better just to make another one worse.

TOP-UP SHOP 8

Most people do just one main grocery shopping trip a week. Surveys have shown that most of us spend 80 per cent of our family food budget in this one trip.

Lots of food goes to waste as a result. More than a third of the food we buy ends up in the bin – some as peelings and offcuts, but a lot simply goes bad in the fridge, cupboard or vegetable rack because we buy too much at once or don't plan ahead and end up with ingredients we never use.

Most of us already visit other shops in between main shopping trips to top up our cupboards with things such as bread and milk that run out or go stale. These 'top-up' visits to the shops tend not to be special trips but instead are done on the way back from work, or in combination with other journeys, so are very efficient and have little impact on the planet.

So, one way to help cut your carbon footprint is to give up the weekly shop and do lots of smaller 'top up' shops instead, fitting them into your regular routine. By doing this you can avoid extra travelling to buy your groceries, and can waste less and eat fresher food as well.

9 EAT LESS PACKAGED FOOD

Despite the popularity of books and television programmes about food (in 2002 alone, more than 900 cookery books were published!), we are actually cooking less. Almost a third of us eat at least one ready meal per week, and sales of ready meals are up around 50 per cent compared with 1990.

Processed, packaged food goes through a lot before it reaches the supermarket shelves. The individual ingredients may have come from many different countries and been transported to a central factory for cooking. After this, the finished product is chilled or frozen, and packaged up in plastic and cardboard before being transported by lorry, via a distribution centre, to the supermarket.

Despite the energy used in cooking, home preparation of meals from raw ingredients often has a lower overall carbon footprint than convenience meals, and this is almost always the case if the meal is feeding more than one person.

Many processed foods also contain high levels of additives, such as colourings, to ensure they still look appetising after a week in the fridge, large amounts of salt (although this is gradually being reduced after pressure from health campaigners) or artificial sweeteners.

Around one fifth of household waste is food packaging, while a lot of packaged food is wasted, partly thanks to the habit of the weekly shop, but also by shops themselves throwing away food that is past its sell-by date.

All these problems can be reduced by shopping for fresh food, and by cooking more meals from scratch.

If you're as busy as me, it's unlikely you'll be able to cook every day. However, there are lots of great recipes that don't take a lot of time, such as quick pasta dishes, salads and fish.

For more involved recipes, cooking large batches when you have time and then putting portions in the freezer to create your own 'ready meals' is a great idea, and means you can make them to your own favourite recipes and avoid additives and too much salt.

EXERCISE YOUR CONSUMER ELBOW

As the famous saying goes, 'the customer is always right', but many companies are holding back on providing greener choices because they don't believe there is enough demand from their customers. After all, the things they have been stocking for years are still being bought, so why should they go to the trouble of changing if they can't see a problem?

A lot of the time, simply telling your local shops that you'd like to see more green, organic or fair-trade products on the shelves will prompt them to think about getting in some new stock. For bigger companies, a letter to their HQ could be all it takes to make a difference, especially if others have the same idea as you.

Exercise your consumer elbow once in a while and there's every chance you'll make a difference, and save yourself time and trouble hunting out greener products in the future as well.

10 ASK FOR WHAT YOU WANT

Your local shops (and bigger stores, too) probably have a lot on their plate, and won't put green issues at the top of their priorities of their own accord. They may actually be delighted to have someone doing their market research for them, and suggesting new products for them to stock.

My local corner shop now has a wide range of FairTrade coffee on its shelves, thanks to enquiries from me and other local people showing the owners there was a strong demand in the area.

If you've looked high and low to find the perfect green product, and then found it online, why not take the packet to your local shops and ask them to get some in? This will save others going to the trouble you went to, and save you time when you next need to stock up as well.

COMPLAIN

Companies do want to please their customers, and a politely worded complaint can often do the trick if you find environmentally unfriendly goods being promoted in the shops when there are better alternatives. If a company has started using environmentally damaging palm oil in your favourite biscuits, writing in to ask them to change back to their original recipe really could make a difference.

Marketing can be another useful thing to complain about. Companies and shops sometimes run promotions with distinctly ungreen prizes, such as tropical holidays and gas-guzzling cars. This sometimes happens when the company is otherwise very green – I've even seen a big 4x4 being offered as a prize by an organic food producer!

Often companies do things like this without thinking, and polite complaints by loyal customers can be more effective than a noisy protest outside company HQ in getting them to change their ways. So, if something in the shops winds you up, help the cause by writing in and asking them to drop a product that does a lot of damage or suggesting a more appropriate prize for their next promotion.

Follow these tips for effective letters that might just make a difference:

• Write to the right person, by name. Find out who the responsible manager, buyer or company director is and write directly to them. You can usually find this information on the company's website. Writing to the correct person will increase the chance of your letter being read and taken seriously, and shows you are serious, too.

• Be polite and constructive. Give the company a clear alternative to what you are complaining about, and suggest different products or a different prize for a future prize draw.

12 START A CAMPAIGN

There are literally hundreds of examples of changes shops have made in response to campaigns led by consumers and professional campaigners.

Setting up a campaign can be as easy as starting a petition on the internet or writing a template letter to a company CEO and asking your friends to pass it around. You can even use free web tools, such as Facebook groups, to collect together support.

While it can take years of pressure to force a company to make a big change in policy, some changes are so simple and easy for companies to do that it can take just a handful of letters from precious customers to make a difference.

Here are just a few examples of successful campaigns to inspire you:

• The FairTrade movement has grown almost exclusively as a result of consumer action. Starting out in the Netherlands in the 1980s, there are now hundreds of FairTrade products giving farmers in developing countries a decent living from producing basic goods such as coffee, tea, cocoa and sugar.

• In response to customer requests for more environmentally friendly underwear, British retailer Marks & Spencer has made a commitment to manufacture more of its cotton basics from organically farmed cotton. Starting out in 2006, the company's new demand for organic cotton caused a temporary shortage on the world market.

• Most recently in 2007 in the UK, chocolate manufacturer Cadbury reintroduced its bubbly chocolate bar, the 'Wispa' which it had stopped making in 2003 after customers mounted an online campaign with e-petitions and groups on social networking websites Facebook, MySpace and Bebo.

• Environmental group Greenpeace is currently pushing shops to stop selling old-style incandescent light bulbs and stock energy-efficient varieties instead. By getting customers to send postcards to the managers of their favourite shops, they have succeeded in getting commitments to phase out the old light bulbs from several major retailers, including Woolworths.

CUT DOWN ON WASTE

A big shopping trip can be a real eye-opener to the problem of packaging waste. You get home with a bunch of new purchases, eager to get them out and look at them, and afterwards you have a small pile of your new stuff and a huge pile of empty bags, boxes and plastic packets that were wrapped around it all.

Christmas can be a similar experience. Once the presents are unwrapped, there's often more packaging to clear up than presents left under the tree.

For more everyday items, it's a real shame that so few products still come in refillable packaging. Luckily you can hunt out a few very green products that work like this, and their use is increasing again. However, there are also a lot of new products that seem to go out of their way to create packaging waste.

There is always recycling but by avoiding disposable goods, reducing the packaging we bring home, and reusing packets and bags ourselves, we can do a lot more to reduce the amount of this waste that needs to be produced in the first place.

13 DON'T GO DISPOSABLE

'Disposable' is a terrible word. As well as encouraging the wasteful use of resources, it also implies that things can be thrown away without consequences. As a green, the growing number of disposable (one-use only) household goods makes my blood boil.

 I recommend you shun all disposable products, whether it's a duster you 'simply throw away', a razor that lasts only a couple of days, or a coffee machine that is designed to use up a thick plastic pod of coffee every time you want a cup (these machines are expensive to run, too, as each pod only makes one cup).

It's when eating our lunch that most of us encounter disposable items – those plastic forks and spoons, available in most takeaway restaurants, sandwich shops, canteens and coffee shops, are often made of plastic that can't easily be recycled, which makes them even worse.

 One simple way to cut down is to take a real fork and spoon into work and keep them in your desk. That way, when you buy a takeaway salad or yogurt, you won't need to pick up any of the plastic variety.

AVOID PACKAGING 14

At the shops, it's best to reduce the amount of waste material you bring home in the first place.

Choose loose food such as fresh fruit and vegetables, and support shops such as local bakeries that make their bread and cakes on site, so don't need to put them in layers of plastic for transportation.

For bigger purchases, keep an eye on the packaging and make sure you recycle any boxes or reuse them around the house.

Your consumer elbow can come in handy here again. If one of your regular purchases has a lot of packaging that frustrates you every time you buy it, write to the company as a loyal customer and suggest they change things.

15 BAGS, BAGS, BAGS

Plastic bags are a major ecological problem. In the UK alone, more than 13 billion are given away in shops every year. Most of these are used once and then thrown away, which fills up our landfill sites, but if they escape into the wider environment they cause even more trouble. Most rubbish in the world's oceans is made of plastic, and bags have been known to injure and kill animals, including turtles, dolphins and sea birds.

The town of Modbury in England only has 1,500 residents, but was going through hundreds of thousands of plastic bags every year. Thanks to an initiative led by local people, they have now become the first town to ban plastic bags, and will instead be providing quality cloth bags for sale instead, as well as paper bags for smaller purchases.

To eliminate unwanted plastic bags from your life, you can follow their example by making sure you always take reusable cloth bags to the shops with you. If a cotton bag is tricky to carry around, string bags and strong silk bags fold up into a tiny space. With one of these in your pocket or handbag, you'll never need to take a plastic bag again.

For trips to the shops that are planned in advance, why not take a proper big shopping bag? These are available in a wide range of fashionable designs, and are much more stylish and comfortable to carry than a nasty old plastic carrier bag.

SHOPPING FOR YOUR HOME

When you are buying things for the home, there's lots of potential for choosing greener options. From electrical goods to carpets and curtains, there are eco-friendly alternatives for everything, saving energy (and money on your bills), reducing pollution (including inside the home) and saving water and resources across the world.

Electricity use in the home has doubled in the past thirty years, mainly because we have so many new gadgets, and thanks to our terrible habit of leaving everything on standby. But energy-saving appliances are available and are getting better all the time.

While we can't all afford to fill our houses with antiques, furnishing the home is a great chance to make use of pre-owned pieces that will be the heirlooms of the future. New items and soft furnishings now also come in a wide range of eco-materials, which are easy to find online, if not on the high street.

16 ELECTRICAL EXCESS

We have so many different electrical gadgets in the average home nowadays – up from seventeen different kinds in the 1970s to thirty seven today.

Microwaves, DVD players and games consoles all have their uses, but they can be a major drain on the electricity supply, especially if they don't have a proper 'off' switch and are left on standby all the time. Try to buy machines with energy-saving functions and low standby power – and always switch off at the plug when you are finished for maximum green stars.

It's not just electricity that causes problems. We all have gadgets we never use taking up cupboard space, so try to think if you really will use that bread-maker, ice-cream machine or electric shoe polisher before you splash out on another gadget. Lots of energy and resources go into making them, and unwanted electronics take up an awful lot of space in our landfill sites, causing terrible pollution thanks to the heavy metals and other chemicals used in their circuits.

By avoiding gadgets you don't need, you can keep the planet cleaner and preserve precious resources, as well as cupboard space.

LOW-POLLUTION GOODS

Many household appliances, such as washing machines and fridges, now come with informative labels that show you exactly how green they are. Choose the best A-rated machines and you will save huge amounts on running costs, since these 'white goods' are responsible for 40 per cent of the electricity we use.

Look out for the European Eco-Label (a flower with the European stars around it), too. This means appliances have been made with less polluting materials and, for washing machines and dishwashers, that they will save water as well.

Switching your light bulbs from wasteful old incandescent bulbs to very efficient fluorescent bulbs is such a good idea. Each one you change will save you more than fifteen times its cost in electricity bills and replacement bulbs over its lifetime.

Check the websites at the end of this book and order bulbs to fit all your lamps today. But don't do what I did for one lamp and order a spare. It's still sitting in the drawer and will be for another few years at least!

18 GET THINGS REPAIRED

We are slowly turning into a throwaway culture, with more than six million tonnes of household gadgets going to landfill every year in Europe alone. This is a complete waste when they contain useful materials that could be recycled, and is also a waste of the energy used to produce them. In a lifetime, the average person will be responsible for 3.3 tonnes of electrical waste.

Many things don't need to be thrown away at all, but could be repaired to last several years more.

We're good at getting big items such as washing machines repaired, but when was the last time you took something small like a toaster to the repair shop? The fact is, it often seems much easier to buy a new toaster for a few pounds, so millions of only slightly broken toasters end up needlessly in the bin.

The way to prevent this first of all is to avoid buying very cheap disposable household items. Invest in something that will last longer and which is built to be repaired, and you'll actually be getting a bargain.

The second thing is to use the skilled repair people in your local area. A lot of independent electrical shops still offer good-value repair services, and they are easy to find using business directories and the internet.

Supporting local businesses is also great for the local economy – spending money that can be spent again in your area, rather than paying a multinational company for a new item that was cheaply made and then shipped across the world.

19 PICK GREENER FURNISHINGS

Home improvements and new furniture are big purchases, intended to last for ages. We also have to live closely with the results, so it's well worth making sure your furnishings are made with the greenest non-toxic materials, and that they have a low carbon footprint as well.

Reused furniture can range from expensive antiques to very cheap 'junk', but every piece you give a new home to means trees that don't have to be cut down, and materials that don't have to be produced again for a new item.

Tips for second-hand furniture:
• Visit antique shops and auctions for smaller items. Many things are not as pricey as you might think.

• Look in classified adverts or on the internet for second-hand goods in your area.

• Charity shops often have pre-owned furniture for sale in excellent condition.

• If you're handy with sandpaper, local junk shops can provide fantastic, stylish bargains in need of a bit of love and care.

Newly made furnishings can be eco-friendly and non-toxic, too. Follow these tips to cut the impact of your home purchases:

• Make sure you aren't supporting unsustainable logging, and instead buy wooden furniture which is certified by the Forest Stewardship Council (FSC).

• Furniture made from reclaimed wood, from old buildings and broken furniture, is more common these days, so look out for this, too, as well as pieces made from recycled plastic and metal.

• Avoid PVC 'lino' and carpets made from synthetic materials for your floor. Attractive, warm, natural floor coverings include bamboo, rubber, real linoleum, jute, sisal, coir and even seagrass.

• Choose curtains, cushions and other household fabrics made from low-impact, hardwearing materials, such as organic cotton, hemp, linen or bamboo.

And don't forget, when you are finished with your furniture, close the loop by making sure it goes to a good home. Pass it on, sell it through the newspaper or internet, or give it to a charity. Many charities need furniture and, if local, will collect it from your house.

DRESSING UP GREEN

Buying clothes can be very confusing if you're a green. The fashion industry is much more complex than the food industry with many more stages of production, all with environmental or ethical pitfalls.

For one simple garment, the fibres must be grown and harvested, then spun and woven into cloth, then dyed, cut and sewn into shape before being transported to the shops. With all this to monitor, certifying a piece of clothing as 'green and ethical' becomes very hard to do.

But this complexity means plenty of ways to make a difference as well. Bringing fair trade and organic approaches into each process could improve the lives of huge numbers of people as well as protect the environment.

Of course, the simplest way to reduce the impact of your wardrobe is by reusing, recycling and repairing existing clothes and materials, but being greener is also a great excuse to reduce your consumption by buying really high-quality goods that will last. In this chapter, I'll also try to make sense of the various ways companies are making new clothes with green credentials.

20 LOVE VINTAGE

Vintage clothing is one of my favourite things. When I was at college in the 1990s, all the clothing from the 1970s suddenly came back into fashion, so we were all going about town in our mums' old platform shoes and skinny jumpers. At that time, the 1980s look was very much out of fashion, but now batwing sleeves and stripy T-shirts are back in style.

In fact, these days it seems like the style of any period from the 1920s onwards is fair game. This is great if you love the fashions of a particular era, or want to have a bit of variety in your wardrobe, but is even better for the planet.

By buying vintage, you can get gorgeous, high-quality clothes for a fraction of the price of new designer garments and, by reusing, you make a real contribution to saving resources and reducing carbon emissions.

The other good news is that the vintage fashion trade is growing fast, with more organised fairs travelling around the country, and a wide range of online sellers. There are even charity shops that specialise in digging out the best vintage clothing from their donations, so you don't have to do all the searching through the racks yourself.

21 | REPAIR AND ADJUST

Two problems that can send us scurrying to the high street for a clothes-buying binge are when something tears, and when we change shape and find our favourite clothes no longer fit properly. Learning to make simple repairs and adjustments can really help to keep those favourite items in use.

These skills can also come in handy if you find a second-hand or vintage item that is almost just right. I regularly buy trousers and skirts that are slightly too big and take them in for a perfect fit.

Don't panic, I don't have particularly good sewing skills but, by keeping the stitches small and on the inside, simple adjustments such as taking an inch off a waistband are well within the careful novice's ability.

If you really can't handle a needle and thread, try your local dry-cleaners. Many of these shops also offer adjustment and repair services – for much less than the cost of a new item.

Another investment that is really worth making is to have shoes repaired regularly. A timely reheeling or a new layer on the sole can save a favourite pair of shoes from wearing out so badly they can't be repaired at all.

BUY RECYCLED 22

Many companies are busy creating a market for clothes made from recycled materials.

These range from skirts created from fashion industry offcuts to restyled suits to fleece jackets made from recycled water bottles.

These are, unfortunately, still rare, but you can find items made from recycled fabrics in shops ranging from designer boutiques to high-street chains.

Look out for advertisements (big companies doing things such as selling a recycled T-shirt tend to shout about it, especially if they aren't very green in other ways) and always check the label.

Searching on the internet can also help to track down items made from recycled materials.

Two of my favourite companies making recycled fashionable are shoe company Terra Plana (which also makes recycled trainers) and From Somewhere, which has just opened a shop in London selling its beautifully styled patchwork clothes.

23 BUY QUALITY

In these times of instantly disposable 'fast fashion' destined for landfill, we all still secretly dream of a wardrobe full of classic, long-lasting clothes, which all match each other. Who wouldn't want to take the hassle out of deciding what to wear in the morning?

While most of us can't afford to kit ourselves out from head to toe in the finest clothes, we can take this approach with some big purchases and save ourselves money in the end. I apply this principle mainly to shoes and winter coats. After several autumns spent in a ragged old worn-out coat from the previous year, wondering why I couldn't just find the same thing in the shops again, I gave up and splashed out on a really good classic black coat from a relatively posh shop, made in Italy.

This was the best bargain I've ever bought. It was stylish and warm, fitted me really well, and lasted three and a half winters before I had to go through the process again.

For basics, such as coats, trousers and shoes, buying fewer of them, but making sure they are high quality and ethical can save a lot of resources and do a lot of good, even if they aren't made with eco-fibres.

24 SWAP

We all have clothes that are great in theory, but which we just don't wear. They might be too big or too small, perhaps they don't suit us as well as we first thought, or maybe they have just seen one too many parties to be taken out again.

Whatever the reason, a great way to rejuvenate your wardrobe, along with those of your friends, is to organise a clothes-swapping party. These are hugely popular at the moment, with party planners adding swap parties to their repertoires and even nightclubs hosting swap nights with the catchphrase: 'Don't expect to go home in the clothes you arrived in'.

Hosting a swap party at home is really simple (although you must make sure all boyfriends, brothers and fathers are out for the evening or they will ruin it with silly comments). Simply invite between four and ten friends, provide them with drinks and snacks and take it in turns to show the clothes you no longer wear. Everyone tries on things that take their fancy, and then takes home anything they want at the end of the night.

Swapping parties are a great way to get new clothes from a trusted second-hand source, and to clear space in your wardrobe at the same time. As long as everyone doesn't arrive by helicopter, it's a fun way to help save the planet, too.

25 GREENER FIBRES

Cotton is the most valuable non-food agricultural product in the world, and one of the most resource-intensive crops – responsible for 16 per cent of global insecticide use. A lot of poor cotton farmers suffer the effects of agricultural chemicals, yet don't make a fair profit from the big clothing companies.

Bringing FairTrade and organic approaches into the cotton industry has the potential to improve the lives of huge numbers of people and protect the environment. Because of the high impact of cotton production, I always buy organic cotton where I can.

However, there are other fibres that have an even lower impact than organic cotton.

Hemp needs very few nutrients and can be grown organically in most areas of the world, even areas prone to drought and flooding. The fibres can be made into a wide range of fabric weights and the plant also produces oil and seeds for food.

Bamboo is a type of grass and is incredibly fast-growing, needing no artificial fertilisers in most places where it is grown. Bamboo can be used for many household articles and can also be made into hard-wearing fabric.

Wool that is produced organically comes from sheep that are not dipped in chemicals and raised on land that is not allowed to be overgrazed, ensuring that organic wool has a very low environmental impact.

26 BUY ETHICAL

Ethical fashion is really taking off. Last year I was invited to speak at a debate called 'Is Green the New Black?' and, if the number of new fashion labels making organic or FairTrade clothes is anything to go by, the fashion for green fashion looks like it's here to stay.

See the back of the book for a wide range of retailers selling green and ethical fashion to suit all budgets.

Unfortunately, the high-street shops where we buy most of our clothes have been slower to catch on. While a handful of stores are introducing green ranges, most clothes they sell are still being made in ways that don't respect either the planet or the rights of the people making them.

Finding out about the origin of high-street clothes can be difficult and most labels don't tell you much. 'Made in' refers only to the place where the final bits were sewn up, not where the crops were grown or the cloth woven.

Ethical labelling schemes can also be confusing. It would be excellent to see global labelling symbols (like washing instructions) that provided information about environmental impact and workers' rights. But, in the meantime, here are some trusted accreditations to look for:

Soil Association organic certification

This logo on natural products, such as food and textiles, means that they have been grown or reared in ways that reflect the best sustainable practice and processed to strict animal welfare and environmental standards.
www.soilassociation.org

Fair Trade Foundation

The FairTrade logo means that the product has been grown with the welfare of the producers and their employees in mind. Farmers and co-operatives will have received a fair price for their crops, and workers will have received a fair wage for picking or processing the product, as well as decent working conditions.
www.fairtrade.org.uk

The Ethical Trading Initiative

Companies signed up to this have joined an alliance of companies, non-governmental organisations and trade unions to produce and implement corporate codes of practice, which cover working conditions in the supply chain for their goods.

There is no guarantee that all goods from a company that is signed up to the initiative will be produced by well-treated workers, but at least they are talking about the problem and aiming to make things better in the future.

www.ethicaltrade.org

Ethiscore

Ethical Consumer magazine has set up a system that assesses products against a range of ethical criteria, including conditions for workers and protecting the environment. Their website has a range of reports available free, as well as a full range for subscribers.

www.ethiscore.org

GREENER HEALTH AND BEAUTY

Potions and products to help our hair, nails and bodies look, smell and feel better are a billion-dollar business. Both men and women want to look 'ten years younger', and the average person spends hundreds of pounds every year on anti-ageing products alone.

Unlike for medicines, labelling and advertising rules for health and beauty products aren't very strict, and many claim to be 'natural' or full of 'herbal extracts' when, in fact, they are made almost entirely from ingredients derived from crude oil. While the first perfumes were made with plant oils, these days 95 per cent of perfume ingredients are synthetic and petrol based.

Lots of problems are caused by packaging and transport, too. Most beauty products come in heavy, liquid form, so transporting them uses up lots of fossil fuels. And excessive fancy packaging is half the selling point of a lot of face creams and perfumes.

Staying clean, fresh and lovely is essential, so it's great that more companies are now taking the lead and producing cosmetics, creams and shampoos with a much lower impact on the planet, and which are healthier for you as well.

These are not always the most obvious products in the shops, and don't have huge advertising budgets. However, with the big companies always persuading us to try their new products and 'improved' formulas, why shouldn't we go and seek out better, greener products to try for ourselves?

With more natural ingredients, green products are more likely to be pleasurable to use, and to be genuinely good for you. Try them and, if you find they suit you, you've got another great way of saving the planet under your belt – and nicer hair or better skin as well.

27 INGREDIENTS TO AVOID

There are literally thousands of ingredients that can be used in cosmetics and bodycare preparations, many of which pose potential hazards.

Each chemical, at the concentrations used in beauty products, is unlikely to cause immediate damage. However, by using a wide range of products every day, you may be exposing yourself to a cocktail of chemicals that will build up to cause sensitivity reactions or disagree with you in other ways.

Washing these chemicals down the drain afterwards is not great news for the health of the environment either.

Every product you can exchange for a safer alternative will help to reduce these risks.

Phthalates

These chemicals are used as softeners and moisturisers to help ingredients penetrate the skin's external layers (not a good thing when combined with other chemicals!). Phthalates are similar to hormones and can harm child development and cause allergies, so they have now been banned from children's toys in the EU and the USA.

These are easily spotted on the label, as they all have the word 'phthalate' in their names.

Fluoride

A toothpaste packed with fluoride isn't the only way to a cleaner, whiter smile. In fact, consuming too much fluoride can actually lead to brown spots on your teeth. If you live in an area where fluoride is added to your water, choosing a toothpaste with more natural ingredients is a good idea.

Fluoride content is listed in the ingredients on all toothpastes, often as sodium fluoride or sodium monofluorophosphate.

Formaldehyde

This is a preservative chemical, often added to shampoos and deodorants, and is found in most nail polishes. It is well known for being an irritant to the eyes and lungs, and can cause sensitisation from frequent exposure.

Beauty products containing formaldehyde must be labelled, so it is relatively simple to avoid this chemical.

28 NATURAL ALTERNATIVES

There are many natural cosmetic ingredients, which are much less toxic and work just as well as the chemical alternatives.

Look out for these ingredients for a greener bathroom.

Natural soap
Soap was invented thousands of years ago and was made with natural oils and alkali salts. There are many manufacturers, both new and traditional, making soap the old-fashioned way using a range of natural perfumes, such as lavender and fruit oils. Some of these smell almost good enough to eat.

Organic shampoos and washes
Real organic products will have proper certification on the back of the label, not just a fancy title, so read the label and look out for genuine organic, plant-based ingredients.

Fluoride-free toothpaste
There are many effective toothpastes in the shops that don't contain fluoride, but do have effective natural anti-bacterial compounds and whiteners. Try baking soda (my favourite), aloe vera, tea tree oil or aniseed for a bit of variety on your toothbrush.

Beeswax
A great alternative to petrol-based waxes in lip balm and lipstick.

CRUELTY FREE

Many cosmetics and toiletries are still routinely tested on animals, even though there are around 10,000 ingredients that have already been shown to be safe for human use. For new ingredients, there are lots of non-animal methods of testing, which are often more accurate, and even cheaper.

So, there's no reason at all to use cosmetics that have been tested on animals, and they are increasingly easy to avoid. The Humane Cosmetic Standard is the international approval system for cruelty-free cosmetics. You can find a long list of approved companies on their website – see the links at the end of the book for more information.

29 CUT THE PACKAGING

Since most products in the shops have the same basic ingredients and functions, a lot of the brand values and desirability of products for our bodies are literally wrapped up in the way the stuff is packaged.

This can lead to some real excesses, such as a tiny squidge of eye cream packed up in a tube, in a box, and then in a plastic package that covers most of a square foot on the shelf.

Do your bit to combat this trend by rewarding companies that don't over-package with your custom. Most eco-beauty manufacturers put all their products in standard shapes and sizes of bottles and rely on their ingredients to make them desirable. Many herbal products found in health food shops also have minimal packaging.

REFILL 30

Another good way to reduce packaging and save money is to get your bottles refilled. Many organic and health shops offer this option – for household cleaners as well as for things such as shampoo.

Alternatively, you can set up your own refilling service at home by buying very large bottles to keep in the cupboard, and using these to refill smaller sizes for every day purposes. Buying in bulk is better value for you as well as being better for the planet.

I was surprised recently to find how many of the perfume counters in my local department store also offer a refill service. This is much cheaper than buying a new bottle of expensive perfume, while saving resources at the same time.

31 | SPRAY LESS

If there is one thing I would un-invent, it would be the aerosol. Although they don't now contain chemicals that damage the ozone layer, the propellant inside (usually butane gas) is still a fossil fuel, which is flammable and rather dangerous.

Aerosols are completely pointless, since there's no job I can think of where an aerosol spray is essential. For jobs where you do want a fine mist, aerosols are far less reliable than a pump bottle, often breaking down with half the product left inside, and you can't repair or reuse them.

Nevertheless, a huge range of beauty and personal care products are still being sold in aerosol cans. Try these alternatives to stamp out spray cans from your daily routine:

• Use roll-on or stick deodorants. Or for a really green option, with no hazardous chemicals, try a crystal deodorant stone. These are just a block of crystal salt containing natural alum. Unlike anti-perspirants containing aluminium, they don't block your pores to stop you sweating, but do kill bacteria effectively to keep you smelling sweet all day – and no white marks!

• If you are a man, use shaving cream or soap and an old-style shaving brush. Both are better for your skin than aerosol shaving foam, and I'm reliably informed that a shaving brush is fab to use.

• Get hairspray in a pump bottle. These are also refillable, unlike aerosols.

GOING OUT GREEN

The things we do in our leisure time account for a surprisingly high proportion of our total energy use. Around 18 per cent of our carbon emissions are created in the process of providing us with opportunities to have fun and if we include catering, this increases to 31 per cent.

This may come as a shock, since most things we do in our spare time don't directly involve burning fossil fuels, but the background activities that go towards keeping us entertained really do add up.

Plenty of these are transport related, whether it's getting food to restaurants or getting ourselves to the multiplex cinema or theme park.

In Aldous Huxley's famous book *Brave New World*, written in the 1930s, he does a marvellous job of predicting all kinds of needlessly wasteful leisure activities. From 'centrifugal bumble puppy' (a mechanised catch game for children) to 'escalator fives' and the 'feelies' (tactile cinemas packed with new technology), everything was designed to use as many resources as possible and keep society busy. The authorities are proud they have conditioned people to love country sports, and then say, 'we see to it that all country sports shall entail the use of elaborate apparatus. So that they consume manufactured articles as well as transport.'

In terms of our leisure activities, we're not far off *Brave New World's* vision these days, staying away from natural activities and spending time and money travelling to centralised passive 'entertainment complexes' instead. Swapping just some of these wasteful activities for simpler pleasures could make a big difference to the planet.

32 BE A GREENER DINER

We have already looked at how to reduce the impact of our food at home, and the same principles of cooking local food in the correct season should apply to restaurants as well. There are more organic and environmentally friendly restaurants opening, but these tend to be rather exclusive and hard to find, so helping and encouraging existing restaurants to be greener is a great way for us to make a difference without abandoning our favourite eateries.

Restaurants may need lots of encouragement – studies have shown that, even among caterers keen to source more of their ingredients locally, reliable local sources of food were hard to find. For a busy small business owner, even a small amount of effort can be enough to put them off, unless they know it will help their business in other ways.

One thing restaurant owners said, when asked why they weren't becoming greener, was that they were rarely asked about the environmental impact of their food by customers and didn't think it was important to them. So, the simple answer is to tell them it is! Talk to the manager of your favourite restaurant, ask them whether they have thought of sourcing more organic and local food, and you might find they are already thinking about it and just need your encouragement to make the change.

For any restaurant, publicity is important, so don't forget to point out that going green is a great thing to put on leaflets and adverts

in the paper to attract new, environmentally conscious diners – and to keep customers like you happy.

Another great suggestion is for restaurants to cut down on bottled water by serving tap water in washable glass bottles or carafes instead.

Bottled water wastes a huge amount of energy being transported around the world and usually comes in non-biodegradable packaging, causing more problems. It's the fastest-growing drink sector in the world with people in the UK alone downing 13 million litres a week.

But there's no need when piped tap water is much more eco-friendly and just as safe to drink.

33 GREENER LEISURE

In theory, leisure time could be some of the greenest hours we spend. What could be more environmentally friendly than taking a walk in the park or kicking a football around on a local sports field?

Have more fun in your spare time by treating yourself to some simpler pleasures now and again and you'll also reduce your carbon footprint.

You'll find there are loads of things on offer in your local area that don't involve lots of travel or lots of complicated machinery. Go to watch your local football or cricket team play (or even join the team), take a long walk to a country pub with a group of friends, support local bands and theatre companies playing in pubs and small venues, go for a bike ride, or join an evening class to learn a new skill or craft and you'll have a great time, make new friends and save carbon, too.

SPECIAL OCCASIONS

Dotted throughout the calendar are days specially made for celebrations. From Christmas and Easter to Valentine's Day, Halloween and, of course, birthdays, these are all good excuses for a party and lots of presents.

Over the years, traditional religious festivals, such as Christmas, have evolved from a simple meal or trip to church into several weeks of non-stop parties and buying stuff. If you're a green, making these celebrations more eco-friendly may seem hard to do – who wants to interrupt the party with a complicated ecological checklist?

But having a greener time, while still having a great time, is possible. The key is to make a few simple changes that don't ruin the fun but actually improve it.

34 TOP TIPS FOR FESTIVALS

Family festivals, such as Christmas, are good for the planet in many ways. For a change, we get together with our friends and family in one house and share tasks like cooking and eating for a few days, reducing our per-person energy use considerably.

However, traditional festivals can very easily become a time of unnecessary excess in many ways, so follow these tips for a greener time:

• For the big meal, get organic free-range meat for the roast, and buy it from a local supplier. Raising organic meat uses far fewer resources, including energy, water and pesticides, and has a much better taste – you will even notice it when you are using up the leftovers.

• Make sure you buy local food for the rest of the menu, and remember to compost the peelings and to recycle bottles and other packaging, too.

• For lighting decorations, invest in LEDs (light-emitting diodes). These use much less energy than traditional bulbs, don't overheat as much, last for years and years without having to change bulbs, and also come with beautiful colour-change functions.

• At Easter, buy FairTrade, organic chocolate for your friends and family. This is often much tastier and a lot 'posher' than normal brands. It's more expensive, but receiving a smaller amount isn't a problem when it tastes that good.

When it's all over, why not work off all that extra food and drink with a spell at the Green Gym? There are conservation projects all over the country, where you can get training and take part in energetic outdoor work that helps the local environment.

35 THROWING PARTIES

Whether you are celebrating your birthday, a new job, passing an exam, moving into a new house or winning a football game, most parties are usually less elaborate and tradition-filled than festivals like Christmas.

In fact, all you usually need to throw a party are a handful of friends and a few drinks. As long as you recycle the bottles afterwards, there's no real green problem with that.

More organised parties can get a bit carbon-heavy, though. And once you get to the stage of flying in ice sculptures from Alaska, the planet starts to raise the alarm.

Most of our parties are somewhere in between these two extremes, and there are some simple ways to keep them green:

• Buy organic drinks, and use local food for snacks and nibbles.

• Decorate with simple, ideally recycled, materials rather than spending a fortune on plastic and foil decorations that will just be thrown away.

• Do recycle everything afterwards, particularly bottles.

• Don't use disposable plates, cutlery and glasses. Most wine shops will lend you glasses for free if you're having a party and buy your drinks from them. Provide finger food and you can avoid plates altogether.

• If you are hiring entertainment, look for one of the growing number of solar-powered sound systems, DJs and bands. Yes, I know most parties are at night! These firms will charge up their equipment during the day before they arrive at your event.

36 HAVE A GREEN BIRTHDAY

A birthday only comes once a year, and making it a special occasion for your child is very important. But whether it's a day out for their friends or a party at home, it is easy to make the day greener and more fun for everyone. It's also a great chance to introduce your child and their friends to greener leisure activities close to home.

For a special day out the kids will be talking about for ages, why not try your local nature reserve? Local Wildlife Trusts have nature parks and reserves all set up for school visits, and many also offer green kids' birthday party events as well. These include activities such as treasure hunts, woodland games and even pond-dipping.

Mixing education and fun is often a challenge, but this kind of muddy, messy outdoor experience does the job brilliantly. With the help of other parents, you could also organise your own nature-based activity day at the beach or in a local wood or park.

For a home party, the old classic games, such as 'pass the parcel' (using recycled wrapping paper from Christmas or a recent birthday) and 'musical chairs' are best, and don't need expensive props or electricity to be enormous fun.

When catering for a kids' party, stay away from sugary snacks (until you get to the birthday cake at the end!) and avoid foods with colourings and other additives, as these can make sensitive children overexcited – not a good idea when they are having an exciting time anyway.

Don't feel that you have to fill plastic party bags with lots of sweets and plastic toys for the kids to take away. Fun recycled bags are easy to make from sticky tape and pages from comics. As well as a piece of cake, put fruit treats inside rather than sweets, and add non-toxic wooden toys or creative gifts, such as coloured pencils.

For decorations, I find it very hard to object to balloons (even the Green Party uses these sometimes), but if you want to be really green, use streamers or bunting instead.

WEDDINGS WITHOUT WASTE

Weddings are really special occasions, and we rightly put a lot of work into getting everything just right on the day.

Like Christmas, weddings used to be simpler affairs. Think of the wedding scene at the end of the famous BBC adaptation of Jane Austen's *Pride and Prejudice*. Despite fussy Mrs Bennett being in charge, there's hardly any bother, no three-year planning process, and the two pairs of love birds simply drive off in carriages straight after the ceremony.

Over the years, we've added numerous extra trimmings to the 'traditional' wedding day, hardly any of which are central to the point of celebrating two people's love and commitment with their closest family and friends.

Organising a modern wedding, with hen and stag weekends, rehearsal dinners, pre-wedding breakfasts and after-ceremony parties in the evening, can lead to a lot of stress and expense, and increase a wedding's impact on the planet. But luckily, plenty of green-minded people are getting married, too, coming up with creative, eco-friendly alternatives and helping to bring about a growing number of green suppliers of wedding essentials.

Follow these tips for a wedding that won't overwork the carbon calculator.

37 CHOOSE GOOD GOLD

Every wedding needs at least one gold ring to symbolise the contract between the bride and groom. But because gold is scarce, even in high-quality ores, mining this precious metal has a big impact on the environment.

The gold for one wedding ring can leave behind 20 tonnes of mining waste. Irresponsible mining companies operating in gold-rich areas can cause huge amounts of water and soil pollution if they let the chemicals used to extract and purify the gold, including cyanide and mercury, leak into the environment.

The simplest answer is to use antique or second-hand rings. These are often unique or come with a story, adding to the romance of the occasion.

Alternatively, you can buy new rings from a jeweller that uses only recycled gold, rather than newly mined metal. Gold tends not to be landfilled anyway, due to its high value, and about 20 per cent of gold on the market already comes from reclaimed or scrap metal. However, this is generally mixed in with new gold and there is no way of knowing where this has come from or how it has been mined.

Green jewellers are increasing in number all the time, and are coming up with new ways to make sure the gold they use is ethical, including sourcing it from old computer parts, and making bespoke rings from old jewellery you provide.

For engagement rings, it is also important to make sure diamonds are not being mined to support conflicts around the world. Look out for stones certified by the Kimberley Process Certification Scheme.

38 FIND A GREEN DRESS

Wedding dresses are usually made to a high standard and with gorgeous materials, but are then only worn once, making a second-hand dress a great way to save resources when planning your wedding without compromising on quality. You can pick up designer dresses for a fraction of their newly made price, and have money left over to hire a dressmaker to adjust it to a perfect fit for you.

There are plenty of sources of vintage and second-hand wedding dresses. Designer dress-exchange shops and agencies can be found in most towns and cities, and the internet has several specialist sites that put buyers and sellers in touch with each other.

If you can't find the perfect pre-worn dress, buying a new dress can still be a green option. Some designers specialise in eco-friendly materials, and most dressmakers will support you if you want to find eco-fabrics for them to use.

See the back of this book for some useful places to look for greener wedding dresses.

For bridesmaids, make sure you provide outfits they can wear again and again. They will be thankful, and the planet will be happy as well.

And for a going-away or evening outfit, why not splash out on a vintage designer suit or cocktail dress? What better excuse to look like Audrey Hepburn for the day?

WEDDING LOCATIONS 39

These days, you aren't confined to a simple choice of church or registry office. Hundreds of venues now have licenses to hold weddings on their premises, from farms to castles.

Combining venues for the wedding and reception saves having to transport all your guests across town. And if the venue also provides accommodation, everything can be in the one place, reducing the amount of organisation you have to do, and making the day less stressful for everyone.

Make sure your caterers source the food from local sources (use an organic farm for the venue and you could reduce the food miles even more) and get organic champagne, wine and other drinks. Some people say drinking organic wine results in less of a hangover, although I have yet to see any evidence of this!

40 MAKE ONLINE INVITES

A beautiful invitation card is hard to leave out of wedding plans, but if your guests are mainly young, an online invite could be a creative alternative.

For a more traditional invitation, there are many environmentally friendly options, with artists and designers making handmade invitations with anything from hemp to sheep dung. If you don't want to experiment with exotic green materials, most traditional wedding stationery companies now offer the option of printing invitations, order of service cards and place markers on 100 per cent recycled paper.

Rather than sending all your guests a thick envelope stuffed with maps, wedding lists and other information, why not set up a website instead? You don't need to be very technical to do this. A simple blog template can be set up very simply in wedding-friendly colours, and can be a great way to keep people up to date on arrangements.

After the wedding, the site can be used to post thank-yous and photos, too.

SET UP GREEN LISTS 41

Setting up a wedding list is an ideal time to, cheekily, introduce your friends and family to greener shopping.

Most people getting married no longer set up a home at the same time, so if you are already well stocked with household goods, you might want to ask people to contribute to a favourite charity instead of buying lots of new stuff.

Many people now choose a hybrid list, with one list on a charity site and one on a shopping site. That way, your guests have a choice, you get some new things you do need, and the planet and less fortunate people get a boost as well.

See the links at the back of this book for places to set up ethical and green wedding lists.

GREENER GIFTS

I find most of my shopping dilemmas occur around Christmas and birthdays. My family tend to be in the 'you shouldn't have' school of present receivers, and have a lot of stuff filling up their houses already. All this makes it a real challenge to get them something that is both useful and planet-friendly at the same time.

Even the most hardened non-consumerist green will face the same problem. Giving gifts at special times is a tradition we shouldn't lose, but with greener giving we can help keep the consumerism in check and make a real difference.

From charitable presents to non-material 'experiences', there are lots of alternatives with a very low carbon footprint. And a gift is a great way to introduce your friends and family to an eco-product they may never have tried otherwise. You never know, you might convert them permanently.

42 CHARITABLE PRESENTS

One of the best new ideas I have come across recently is the totally charitable gift. By this I don't mean FairTrade products (though they are nice, too), but the kind of gift where you give money to a charity that's enough for them to achieve something tangible in the area where they work.

The charity Oxfam pioneered this idea with their 'Unwrapped' gift programme, and they still have one of the best selections. For the gift you choose, they send a card to the recipient that says what your donation is able to achieve, along with a cute picture of a goat, farm, school dinners, and so on.

There is an enormous number of different things to choose across a wide range of charities, and these are just a few examples:

• Books for a schoolchild
• A cow or goat for a poor farmer
• Planting a new hedgerow
• Music lessons for disadvantaged children close to home
• Training in workers' rights for women in factories
• A beehive
• A shelter for use in big emergencies

Find a range of charity gift schemes at the end of this book.

NON-MATERIAL GIFTS 43

For people with plenty of clutter already, why not give something non-material that doesn't have a huge carbon footprint and doesn't need a lot of wrapping paper?

For this kind of gift, you aren't restricted to shops and services with existing voucher schemes or formal tickets. Putting together your own custom 'voucher' using your artistic skills or your computer can add a personal touch and open up lots of new possibilities.

And for things that aren't nearby, don't forget to get a train ticket as well!

Ideas include:
• Tickets to a local theatre
• A trip to see their favourite band or football team
• Dinner at a local restaurant.
• A visit to an art gallery or museum
• A voucher for a massage or some aromatherapy
• An offer to dig the garden or do their ironing for a week

44 GET ECO-GADGETS

Some gadgets are genuinely useful or educational, and can help people with their energy saving or stimulate an interest in green issues they never knew they had.

For tech-y people, my top gadget is a home electricity meter monitor (brands include Electrisave and Efergy), which provides a portable readout of their electricity meter.

With one of these gadgets, saving energy actually becomes fun, as you can walk around the house and check the impact on the reading of different pieces of equipment. It's also a great reminder to turn things off at the end of the day. The novelty doesn't seem to wear off, as people with these have been shown to save up to 25 per cent on their electricity bills.

More down to earth are a set of eco balls for the washing machine. There are various different brands, available from most online eco-stores and some high-street shops.

They all work by creating molecules in the water that help remove dirt without the chemicals usually used in washing powder. Don't ask me for a full scientific explanation (they do need refilling once every several hundred washes, so there must be something going on inside them), but they really do work and save a fortune on washing bills.

These are a great gift as most people wouldn't try of their own accord, but once they have them, are quickly converted.

GREEN DESIRABLES 45

There are some items we all need, so buying these as gifts is hardly consumerism gone mad and is unlikely to be considered unnecessary clutter by your loved ones either.

Although these aren't as exciting as eco-gadgets, almost everyone I know would appreciate being given these essential items as gifts:

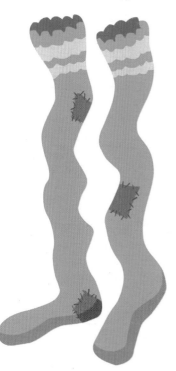

- Towels made from eco-friendly fabrics, such as hemp or organic cotton

- Recycled stationery items, such as pencils, pens and notebooks

- Socks made from soft, breathable green fabrics

- FairTrade coffee and tea (and chocolate, though that's not strictly an essential!)

- Organic jams and sauces from local shops and markets (these are often packaged attractively, too)

GREEN BABIES

There's a lot to sort out when you have a baby on the way. Considering babies are so small and have such simple needs, it's amazing what a shopping frenzy expectant parents can get into, costing them a fortune as well as adding to the stress of a new arrival.

Babies grow up surprisingly quickly, so a lot of these purchases will only be used a few times before the little one gets too big for them.

While keeping an eye on the carbon footprint of your new family is important, another major worry for parents centres around keeping babies away from toxic chemicals and other ingredients in food, clothes and toys.

Having a greener baby doesn't have to be complicated. Here are lots of easy tips on creating a non-toxic, low-carbon world for your offspring.

46 FEED BABY GREEN FOOD

For the first few months, you will either be feeding your baby with breast milk (best for baby, and it's free) or with formula milk. If you are using formula, look for organic mixes and avoid brands that market themselves aggressively in the developing world, where dirty water supplies make breastfeeding by far the safest option.

Once your baby is starting on real food, it can be tempting to rely solely on jars of pre-made food. There are many organic brands on the market (around half of baby food sales are now organic), but this is expensive and leaves lots of jars to recycle as well.

By making your own baby food from a variety of real, fresh ingredients, you will know exactly what your baby is getting and will save money and waste as well.

Your freezer is a great place to create a well-stocked baby food store. Whizz up a range of dishes in batches, then freeze them in ice-cube trays or small plastic containers from which you can also serve the food. Mealtimes are then a simple case of choosing one from the freezer, defrosting and reheating in the microwave.

47 LOW-CARBON CLOTHES

It's so tempting to dress up your cute little baby in the latest designer wear, but the rate they go through clothes means each baby outfit won't enjoy many outings before it's too small.

If everyone bought a full complement of new baby clothes and then threw them all away, an awful lot of high-quality goods would go to waste. But, luckily, there are lots of people who have been in this boat before, so there are plenty of places to find gorgeous pre-worn baby clothes.

I'm very proud of the 'hand-me-downs' I'm wearing in my baby photos, from beautiful print dresses to my favourite: a fantastic flared 1970s boiler suit that I was never out of until it got too small.

If you haven't got friends with cupboards full of outgrown classics, recycling websites, such as Freecycle, are great sources of baby clothes.

For new items, the most important thing is to get fabrics that don't contain toxic chemicals. Organic cotton and hemp have a low impact on the planet and are great for sensitive baby skins. Bamboo baby clothes are very hardwearing and increasingly popular, too.

See the section at the end of this book for some great places to get natural baby clothes.

KEEP BABY ECO-CLEAN 48

Baby skin is new and soft, and can be very sensitive to harsh chemicals in washes, soaps, creams and other cleaning products.

Avoid highly perfumed soaps and shampoos made with petrochemicals and go for plant-based, biodegradable versions instead. These are kinder on the skin and they break down more easily in the environment, reducing pollution.

Try simple olive oil to soften skin instead of perfumed baby lotion, and use bottom wipes made without perfumes or propylene glycol (a petrol-based ingredient in antifreeze).

When washing baby clothes (and nappies), it's even more important to use a mild, eco-friendly washing powder.

49 BOTTOM BUSINESS

Nappies are a major issue for green-minded parents, simply because of the sheer number of times a baby has to be changed in its first couple of years.

From when it is born until it gets the hang of potty training, the typical baby goes through more than 5,000 nappies. In the UK, nine million disposable nappies get put in landfill every day. In America, this is forty-nine million, and each nappy will take hundreds of years to fully decompose.

'Real' or washable nappies have changed a lot since I was little, and they are growing in popularity once again. You can get real nappies, liners and supplies from major supermarkets now, not just specialist suppliers.

The fact is, real nappies are nothing to be scared of. With modern designs, liners and wraps, leaks are even rarer than with disposables, and there isn't a safety pin in sight.

The environmental savings come in two parts: lower use of resources and energy savings.

The biggest of these is cutting down on the waste you generate. Using mainly real nappies cuts out almost all the landfill impact of disposables. Energy savings aren't as dramatic, since real nappies do need to be washed a lot. However, a study that compared boil-washing real nappies with the energy involved in making disposables over a baby's first few years found a small saving in energy.

In real life, you can actually do a lot better than this by not using a boil wash. This is not necessary at all – sixty degrees is plenty hot enough.

You can save even more energy by using a nappy laundry service, which can be found in most towns and, because they save you lots of work as well, they can be very good value.

Do get advice on real nappies from people who have used them successfully and do try them out before you buy a whole kit. Also look out for incentive schemes in your local area, which can provide grants to help with the initial expense of buying the nappies.

Overall, real nappies are greener and much cheaper than disposables, coming in at less than half the cost from birth to potty.

Greener disposables

A mixture of real nappies and disposables suits a lot of green parents, and most real nappy users buy disposables for certain occasions.

On a trip where several changes will be needed, a stock of greener disposables can be very useful, so you don't need to carry all the soiled nappies around with you until you get home.

Eco-friendly disposables are more biodegradable and are made with natural materials, leaving out chemicals such as deodorants and bleach. Absorbency is increased with natural materials, such as corn starch, rather than synthetic gels.

More information about real nappies and greener disposables can be found via the organisations listed at the back of this book.

50 BABY BITS AND PIECES

Even if you try to keep baby-related shopping to a minimum, you will still find your shopping list gets very full of gadgets, furniture and other items you need to make your baby feel at home.

Most of these bits and pieces are built to last, but will only be in use for a few months, so buying second-hand or swapping with friends are both great ways to save money and resources. And don't forget, once your little one has grown out of them, to pass them onto the next set of shopped-out parents, too.

The only used items you really shouldn't buy second-hand are car safety seats and mattresses. Everything else can be recycled several times over.

Designers are catching up with the need for eco-friendly baby accessories and you can now find baby furniture which is multi-purpose – turning from a cot to a proper bed or from a changing table to a craft table later on.

For toys for very young babies, new and non-toxic is best, and a wide range of natural wooden toys and organic teddy bears are available now.

As they grow up and start taking everything apart, second-hand toys can be great value. You can pick up vast quantities of used plastic building bricks for next to nothing in charity shops or on the internet – after a good wash these are as good as new. My nephew has by far the longest racing track around, thanks to a combination of new parts and a huge old collection of track sections from our attic (most of which were second-hand when we got them, too).

Plastics are usually made from petroleum and other chemicals. When new, they will 'off gas' some of these chemicals for several months, so second-hand plastic toys can pose fewer health hazards as well.

MORE INFORMATION, TIPS AND SHOPS

Think local

You'll find the best local shops by stepping away from the computer and exploring your local area to find the hidden gems.

For organic food and drink, the Organic Store provides a directory of stockists in the UK. Simply click on your local area to find those nearest to you.
www.organic-store.co.uk

Find a farmers' market near you at the National Association of Farmers' Markets.
www.farmersmarkets.net

Get online

Ebay – online auctions to sell and buy second-hand bargains
www.ebay.co.uk

Freecycle – find your local group and register to look for free things in your area, or to find a good home for your unwanted items.
www.freecycle.org/group/

Craigslist – the original and best online classified ads. This address should redirect you to your local listings.
www.craigslist.org

Online shops are great for green stuff that's hard to find on the high street. Here are some of my favourites.

Natural Collection
www.naturalcollection.com

Nigel's Eco Store
www.nigelsecostore.com

Ecotopia
www.ecotopia.co.uk

The Green Shop
www.greenshop.co.uk

The Green Store
www.thegreenstoreonline.co.uk

Centre for Alternative Technology shop
www2.cat.org.uk/shopping

WWF's Earthly Goods shop
shop.www.org.uk

For a wider range of different companies, including small local suppliers, look at the Ethical Junction website, which lists literally hundreds of green and ethical suppliers.
www.ethical-junction.org

Shopping for your home

Find antiques fairs and local auction houses at the UK Auction Guides:
www.ukauctionguides.co.uk

Some great sources of greener furnishings and fabrics:

www.organic-furnishings.co.uk
www.naturalhome-products.com
www.greenfibres.com
www.thegreenhaus.co.uk
www.greengreenhome.co.uk
www.ecocentric.co.uk
www.traidcraftshop.co.uk

Dressing up green

One of the best green fashion sites around is Style Will Save Us. They specialise in the latest news on how to find great vintage fashion at fairs around the country.
www.stylewillsaveus.com

Most vintage clothes sellers are small and sell online as well as from their specialist shops. Try putting 'vintage fashion' and your location into a search engine, and many quality sellers will come to light.

If you are visiting London, the best place for fashionable second-hand clothes is still Camden Town. The Lock Market and Stables Market have racks and racks of quality cast-offs.
www.camdenlock.net

Living Ethically has an excellent shopping section, where you can find local shops throughout the UK stocking green and fair-trade fashion.
www.livingethically.co.uk

Other shops and suppliers of greener clothing:

Get ethical fashion, books, gadgets, advice and more from the Ethics Girls Website
www.ethicsgirls.co.uk

Adili stocks clothes from a range of green labels and designers.
www.adili.com

People Tree – the original fair-trade clothing label
www.peopletree.co.uk

Terra Plana/Worn Again (shoes and trainers)
www.terraplana.com

Boutique with stylish clothes made from recycled offcuts.
www.fromsomewhere.co.uk

The Hemp Trading Company – urban clothing made from eco-friendly hemp.
www.thtc.co.uk

Howies in South Wales makes some of my favourite organic casual clothes
www.howies.co.uk

Green and ethical certification schemes:

Soil Association (organic certification)
www.soilassociation.org

The Fairtrade Foundation:
www.fairtrade.org.uk

The Ethical Trading Initiative, where unions, charities and companies work together to develop better standards for workers around the world.
www.ethicaltrade.org

Ethical Consumer magazine hosts the ethiscore website, where you can look up green and ethical ratings for a wide range of products. There are plenty of free reports available online, or you can subscribe for wider coverage.
www.ethiscore.org

Greener health and beauty

Find lots of natural products in your local health food store.

Aveda stores are spreading fast. Find your nearest shop here:
www.aveda.co.uk

Or try these online stockists:
www.greenpeople.co.uk
www.oliveorganic.com

For cruelty-free (and often green) cosmetics, check the list of approved Humane Cosmetic Standard companies on the website of the European Coalition to End Animal Experiments.
www.eceae.org

Going out green

Finding existing eco-friendly restaurants in the UK isn't simple. VeggieHeaven (www.veggieheaven.com) has a searchable guide and lots of reviews of vegetarian restaurants, many of which have green credentials.

In the USA, the Green Restaurant Association has a searchable database of accredited greener restaurants.
www.dinegreen.com

Special occasions

The Wildlife Trusts have nature reserves all over the country, and many offer eco-friendly back-to-nature birthday parties for kids, or will let you bring a group of children for a fun birthday trip. www.wildlifetrusts.org

Find eco-friendly stocking fillers and party gifts at Toys to You. www.toys-to-you.co.uk

The British Trust for Conservation Volunteers offers 'Green Gym' sessions.
www2.btcv.org.uk/display/greengym

Weddings without waste

The Kimberley Process certifies conflict-free diamonds. www.kimberleyprocess.com

Find hundreds of once-worn and never-worn dresses via the Dressmarket.
www.thedressmarket.net

Organic drinks suppliers

Vintage Roots
www.vintageroots.co.uk

Festival Wines
www.festivalwines.co.uk

Greener gifts

These shops and charities also provide wedding list services for a more ethical wedding. See also the online shops above (and the baby shops below) for more.

Get greener gadgets galore at EcoGadgets.
www.eco-gadgets.com

For your wedding list, Green Fibres has lots of household essentials including towels and bed linen.
www.greenfibres.com

Charity gifts

Oxfam lets you buy charity gifts via their 'unwrapped' website.
www.oxfamunwrapped.com

Good Gifts has a huge range of charitable gifts from home and abroad.
www.goodgiftsshop.org

The Send a Cow charity specialises in livestock and farming-related gifts.
www.sendacowgifts.org.uk

The Charity Gifts website lets you search through a range of charities for the perfect charity gift.
www.charitygifts.com

Wedding List Giving will help enable your wedding guests to give directly to a charity of your choice.
www.weddinglistgiving.com

Green babies

Many of the green clothing suppliers listed above will also stock a wide range of baby clothes and accessories.

Other places to find eco-friendly baby clothes:

www.bamboo-baby.co.uk
www.spiritofnature.co.uk
www.ethicalbabe.com
www.earthlets.co.uk
www.naturebotts.co.uk
www.purbebe.com (USA-based)

The Real Nappy Campaign has a nappy finder service to help you track down incentive schemes, laundry services and shops.
www.realnappycampaign.com